WELCOME TO MY COUNTRY

Welcome to
AUSTRALIA

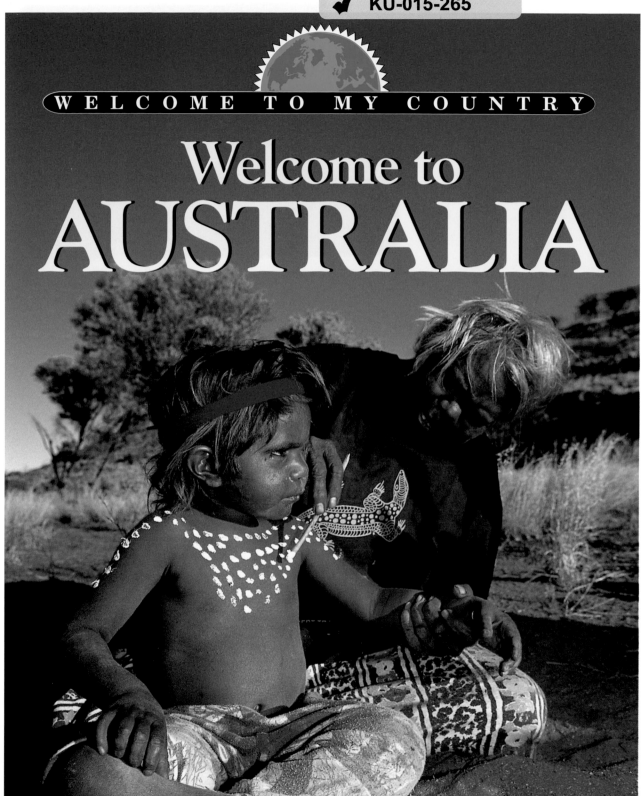

FRANKLIN WATTS
LONDON•SYDNEY

This edition first published in 2005 by
Franklin Watts
96 Leonard Street
London EC2A 4XD

Franklin Watts Australia
45-51 Huntley Street
Alexandria NSW 2015

This edition is published for sale only in the United Kingdom & Eire.

© Marshall Cavendish International (Asia) Pte Ltd 2005
Originated and designed by Times Editions–Marshall Cavendish
an imprint of Marshall Cavendish International (Asia) Pte Ltd
A member of the Times Publishing Group
Times Centre, 1 New Industrial Road
Singapore 536196

Written by: Peter North & Susan McKay
Editor: Melvin Neo
Designer: Geoslyn Lim
Picture researcher: Susan Jane Manuel

A CIP catalogue record for this book
is available from the British Library.

ISBN 0 7496 6017 1

Printed in Singapore

PICTURE CREDITS
ANA Press Agency: 3 (centre), 24, 30
Peter Andrews: 17, 39
Art Directors & TRIP Photographic Library: 26
Camera Press Ltd: 8 (bottom), 13, 32, 33,
    37 (both)
Hoa-Qui: 3 (top), 6, 8 (top), 21, 25, 34, 40
Dave G. Houser/Houserstock: 9, 27, 31, 36
The Hutchison Library: 1, 4
Richard I'Anson: 23, 41, 45
Life File Photo Library: 7 (bottom), 16, 28, 35
Photobank Singapore: cover, 2, 3 (bottom),
    5, 7 (top), 10, 18
Topham Picturepoint: 11, 12, 14, 15 (both),
    19, 20, 29 (both), 38
Travel Ink: cover, 22

Digital Scanning by Superskill Graphics Pte Ltd

Contents

5 **Welcome to Australia!**

6 **The Land**

10 **History**

16 **Government and the Economy**

20 **People and Lifestyle**

28 **Language**

30 **Arts**

34 **Leisure**

40 **Food**

42 **Map**

44 **Quick Facts**

46 **Glossary**

47 **Books, Videos, Web Sites**

48 **Index**

Words that appear in the glossary are printed in **boldface** type the first time they occur in the text.

Welcome to Australia!

Many people imagine Australia as a large island with good weather all year round. More than half the country is covered in desert, but Australia has **temperate** and **tropical** climates too. Let's learn all about the country called "**down under**" and the history of the people who live there.

Opposite: A park guide cares for an orphaned kangaroo.

Below: Most Australian cities are along the coast, so the beach is never far away!

The Flag of Australia

The Australian flag carries the stars of the Southern Cross. This **constellation** is only visible in the **Southern Hemisphere** where Australia is located. The flag of the **United Kingdom** appears in the top left corner.

The Land

Australia is almost as large as the United States, excluding Alaska. Most people live in the big cities around the edges of the country. Sydney, Melbourne, Brisbane and Perth are all located along the Australian coast. The land formations change from region to region. Hardly anyone lives in the dry, central region called the **outback**, or **bush**, which is called the "Dead Heart".

Below: Uluru, or Ayers Rock, is a large sandstone rock in the Northern Territory. It is a sacred site for the **Aborigines**, Australia's original inhabitants.

The eastern and southern coasts, northern Australia and the southwestern region have rich, fertile land that is good for farming.

Most of Australia is very flat. The highest mountain is Mount Kosciusko at 2,228 metres. It is located in the Great Dividing Range which runs along the eastern coast.

The Murray is the longest river in Australia. It snakes through the state of New South Wales, collecting rainfall off the mountain slopes.

Above: The Great Barrier Reef is the world's largest coral reef. Corals live in warm, clear waters, such as those off the shores of tropical Queensland.

Left: Spring flowers cover the land in Western Australia.

Seasons

Australia lies in the Southern Hemisphere, where summer lasts from December to February. The climates of different regions range from dry and hot, to mild and wet.

Above: This giant termite mound is made of mud. It is home to millions of termites — tiny ant-like insects that feed on wood.

Left: In Australia's deserts, many flowers bloom after heavy rains. The land can suddenly burst into a display of beautiful colour.

Plants and Animals

Australia's famous animals include kangaroos, koalas and opossums. These mammals are known as **marsupials**. The mothers carry their babies in a pouch for months.

Special features help Australia's plants survive in its dry climate. Long roots help the eucalyptus tree seek out water. The baobab tree stores water in its thick trunk.

Above: It would take several people to form a ring around the thick trunk of this baobab tree!

History

Australia's Original Settlers

The Aborigines came from Asia about 40,000 to 50,000 years ago and were the first people to settle in Australia. The men hunted land animals and fished. The women gathered seeds, roots and berries. When the Europeans first arrived, there were about half a million Aborigines living across Australia.

Below: Boomerangs are V-shaped objects used by Aboriginal hunters.

The Europeans Arrive

Just over two hundred years ago, European sailors landed on the coasts of Australia. In 1770, British explorer James Cook claimed the eastern coast of Australia for his king, George III. For many years afterwards, Britain sent **convicts** there. New settlements were also established on the southern coast of Australia and on the island of Tasmania.

Above: In 1788, the British raised their flag at Sydney Cove.

A Land of New Possibilities

Before long, **immigrants** were coming to Australia in large numbers, mainly from England and Ireland. These immigrants introduced new ways of farming and mining. They even brought a new animal with them in 1810—the sheep! Soon, Australia was a rich country with a successful wool industry. Australia had become a land with many new possibilities.

Above: In the early 1800s, the new settlers began exploring Australia on camels.

The Commonwealth of Australia

At the beginning of the twentieth century, there were six Australian territories, called colonies, inhabited by immigrants. In 1901, they joined to form a **federation** called the Commonwealth of Australia. Australia still had strong links with Britain, and Australians fought alongside the British in World Wars I and II. The Australian and New Zealand soldiers who fought in the World Wars were called ANZACs.

Left: This memorial in Brisbane is dedicated to the ANZAC soldiers who died fighting during World War I.

Immigration

Since World War II, Australia has encouraged immigration. Today, Australia is known as an immigrant country because many people living there were born elsewhere.

Matthew Flinders (1774–1814)

Matthew Flinders was a famous English explorer. In 1801, he proved that Australia was a single landmass by sailing all the way around the coast. At that time, Australia was known as **New Holland**. He suggested renaming it *Australia,* from the Latin word *australis,* meaning "southern".

Matthew Flinders

Caroline Chisholm (1808–1877)

In the early 1800s, poor women from Britain came to Australia to find a better life. Many of them had no money and lived on the streets. Caroline Chisholm set up the Female Immigrants' Home to help those women. Soon, she was known across the country as "the immigrant's friend". She helped more than ten thousand women.

Caroline Chisholm

Government and the Economy

Government

Australia is divided into six states and two territories. Its government is divided into three sections — the town and city councils, the state and territory governments, and the federal government, which is based in Canberra, the capital city.

Below: The old Parliament House is in Canberra, the capital city of Australia.

Australia's government is run by two houses of elected members — the House of Representatives and the Senate. Together, they decide on laws and government policies. The **prime minister** is the leader of the government and the country. He or she chooses politicians from either house to form a group called the **cabinet**. Each cabinet member, called a minister, is in charge of one area of government. These ministers advise the prime minister.

Agriculture

In the 1800s, the main industry in Australia was sheep farming. Today, Australia is still the world's largest wool-producing country. Cattle farming is important too and produces beef for both the nation and for export. Some cattle stations stretch for miles and miles. Teams of men, trucks and even helicopters are used to round up the herds.

Above: Cattle are brought together into a pen by herders at cattle stations before they are sold.

Industry

In the nineteenth century, ships took months to bring goods to Australia, forcing Australians to make the things they needed for themselves. The Australian manufacturing industry began in this way.

Mining

Australia contains many natural resources. Gold, coal, iron ore, copper and nickel are mined in many regions. Under the ocean, natural gas is drilled and sold to other countries.

Left: Iron ore is one of the major minerals found in Western Australia, along with gold, tin, coal and diamonds.

People and Lifestyle

More Travellers Arrive!

Since the first settlers arrived, many immigrants have moved to Australia. Most people emigrated from Britain, but others travelled from Italy, Greece, China, Vietnam and Lebanon. The original people of Australia, the Aborigines, make up a very small part of the population.

Below: Immigrant Australians and Aborigines have not always been friends, but the situation has begun to improve.

A Melting Pot

In Australia, many races of people live together in one land. The government has introduced a **policy** called "**multi-culturalism**", which encourages ethnic groups to live peacefully with one another.

Many immigrants from Asian countries arrived in Australia in the 1970s. Today, most Australian cities have large Asian communities.

Above: Many Chinese immigrants live in the part of Sydney called Chinatown.

Family Life

Most Australians live in homes in a town or city not far from the coast. Outdoor activities are popular with Australians, and the sunny climate allows them to visit the beach as often as they can.

Left: Going to the beach is a favourite weekend activity. Most children learn to swim when they are very young.

Australia is a big country with a fairly small population, so most of the houses in the cities are large, with gardens at the front and back. Neighbourhoods are friendly, and most people know each other.

Australians are proud of their homes, and they take care of them well. Weekend projects might include painting a fence, mowing the lawn or working in the garden.

Above: Home improvement is a typical Sunday afternoon chore in Australia.

Education

All Australian children must attend school, starting at either five or six years of age. They attend primary school and secondary school. Primary school lasts six years. Students then go to secondary school, which lasts another six years.

Most schools in the country are run by the government and are free. Some parents send their children to private schools which charge a fee.

Below: Children who live in **rural** areas must take a bus to and from school.

After secondary school, students can further their education by attending technical institutions, community colleges or universities.

Australian schools offer activities, such as drama, debating and music, after school. Sports are also popular. Students can join clubs to play Australian Rules football, hockey, netball and cricket. Australian Rules football is also called "Aussie Rules" and has elements of soccer, rugby and basketball.

Religion

Christianity came to Australia with the European settlers, and it is the main religion in the country today.

Before the Europeans arrived, the Aborigines practised their own religion. They believed the spirits of their ancestors lived in the trees, water holes and rocks. Some Aborigines today still hold this belief.

Below: These poles, decorated with carvings and paintings, are placed around Aboriginal graves to honour family members.

The Arrival of Christianity

The Europeans brought Christian beliefs with them from other countries and built churches all over Australia. Some of the first buildings in a town were churches. Immigrants from other countries brought their own religions too. **Passover**, a Jewish festival, is also celebrated. Today, there are Hindus, Buddhists and Sikhs in Australia.

Above: Sydney has many churches. This is St. Mary's Cathedral.

Language

A Mixed Language

The main Australian language is English, spoken by most citizens with an accent handed down by the original settlers from England and Ireland. Immigrants from European and Asian countries brought their own languages with them. Over the years, Australians have adopted some Aboriginal words, such as *Illawarra,* meaning "place by the sea".

Below:
This beach sign is in English, Italian, Spanish, Russian, Vietnamese and Chinese.

Australian Stories

Traditional Australian stories tell of the lives of the people who lived in the outback. A man named A. B. "Banjo" Paterson wrote interesting stories about the outback. He also wrote Australia's unofficial anthem *Waltzing Matilda*.

The stories of the outback are still being told by modern-day writers, such as Australian Colleen McCullough. She wrote the best-selling book *The Thorn Birds*.

Above, left:
In 1973, Patrick White was the first Australian to win the Nobel Prize for Literature.

Above, right:
Peter Carey won the 1988 Booker Prize for Fiction for his book *Oscar and Lucinda*.

Arts

Painting

The oldest paintings in Australia were done by the Aborigines. They decorated cave walls with pictures of animals and people using natural materials such as charcoal.

European settlers brought their own style of painting to Australia. Many famous Australian artists now mix the two styles together.

Below: The colours of this cave painting are typical of Aboriginal art.

Architecture

The Harbour Bridge and the Sydney Opera House are two of Australia's most famous structures. Sydney Harbour is divided by a waterway. The Harbour Bridge joins the two halves of the harbour together.

The Sydney Opera House is one of the busiest theatres in the world, presenting plays, operas, musicals and ballets. Architects and craftspeople took fourteen years to complete it.

Above: The Sydney Opera House is in front of the Harbour Bridge. People in Sydney call the bridge "The Coat Hanger" because of its unusual shape.

Music

Australians love making music! Have you heard of the rock bands the Bee Gees, AC/DC, Midnight Oil and INXS? Or how about the opera singers Dame Nellie Melba and Dame Joan Sutherland, known as two of the world's best performers? These musical stars all come from Australia.

Left: Dame Joan Sutherland sang in operas in Venice, Paris, Milan and New York, as well as in her hometown, Sydney.

Australian Films

The film *Babe: Pig in the City* is the most recent Australian movie to be an international box office hit. *Crocodile Dundee*, about an outback man who moves to New York City, is probably the best-known Australian film.

Many locally produced movies are made in Australia. Every year, Australian filmmakers go to the Cannes Film Festival in France to show their films.

Above: *Crocodile Dundee* was filmed in Australia and the United States. The movie's lead actor, Paul Hogan, is a native Australian.

Leisure

A Love of the Outdoors

Australia's climate is perfect for spending time outdoors. Australians love to watch and play sports, such as cricket and Australian Rules football. Fishing is a very popular Australian pastime. It gives people a chance to get away from the hustle and bustle of the city. The great thing is, the water is never far away!

Below: The waters of the Northern Territory are popular with fishing fans.

Outdoor Adventures

Many Australians like to go **bush-walking**, and there are trails throughout most of the country.

Most Australians live near the coast. They love swimming and surfing. The country is surrounded by water, and there are plenty of great surfing spots on the coast. There is even a beach in Australia called Surfer's Paradise!

Above: Cape York Peninsula is one of the wildest areas in Australia. It is a great place to go bush-walking.

Sports

Cricket is one of the best-loved sports in Australia. Children and adults play this game in backyards, fields and **sporting ovals**. Australian Rules football is the main winter sport.

Horse racing is also a popular spectator sport. The Melbourne Cup horse race, held in November, is the biggest horse racing event in Australia.

Below: On Melbourne Cup day, the racecourse is packed with excited spectators. In the rest of the country, people watch the race on television.

Australian Champions

One of the most famous Australian sports champions is golfer Greg Norman. In 1971, Yvonne Cawley became the first Aboriginal tennis player to win the Wimbledon championship. She won it again in 1980. Pat Rafter won the 1997 U.S. Open Tennis Championship. Aborigine Cathy Freeman won a gold medal in the 400-metre run at the 2000 Olympics in Sydney.

Above, left: Tennis player Yvonne Cawley was a winner at Wimbledon in 1971 and 1980.

Above, right: Golfer Greg Norman has won many international competitions.

Holidays

Christmas is the biggest holiday in the Australian calendar. It falls at the beginning of summer and marks the end of the school year. Most people celebrate the holiday with a family lunch of turkey. Some people celebrate with a barbecue on the beach.

ANZAC Day is on 25 April. It is a day to remember the ANZAC soldiers who lost their lives in war. **Veteran** soldiers parade through the streets wearing their uniforms.

Left: The ANZAC Day parade. These nurses are wearing a sprig of rosemary, the herb of remembrance, above their medals.

Australia Day is celebrated on 26 January. It marks the day the first group of immigrants arrived in the country. People all over Australia celebrate by singing the national anthem and setting off fireworks!

Every year, each state holds an agricultural show. Prizes are awarded for the best cows, the biggest bulls and the sheep with the finest **fleece**. Other contests include the log chop and the high pole, where loggers race to chop the top off tree trunks while balancing on narrow planks.

Above: The log chop is a race to see who can chop a log in half the quickest.

Food

Immigrants brought national dishes with them, and today foods from many other countries are available — pasta from Italy, olives from Greece, curries from India and **kebabs** from Turkey. Recently, traditional Aboriginal foods have also become popular.

Left:
This Aboriginal woman is holding a *wichetty grub*. These fat, white, slug-like creatures are popular in trendy Sydney restaurants!

In the outback, food is very simple. One type of traditional food is **damper**. Damper is flour and sugar mixed with water, cooked over an open fire.

During the summer, many Australians cook on a barbecue pit. They call it a *barbie*. The most popular barbecued foods are meats and seafood. Barbecued vegetables are delicious, too. A barbecue on the beach is a popular way to celebrate Christmas.

Above: There are plenty of public barbecue pits in Australia.

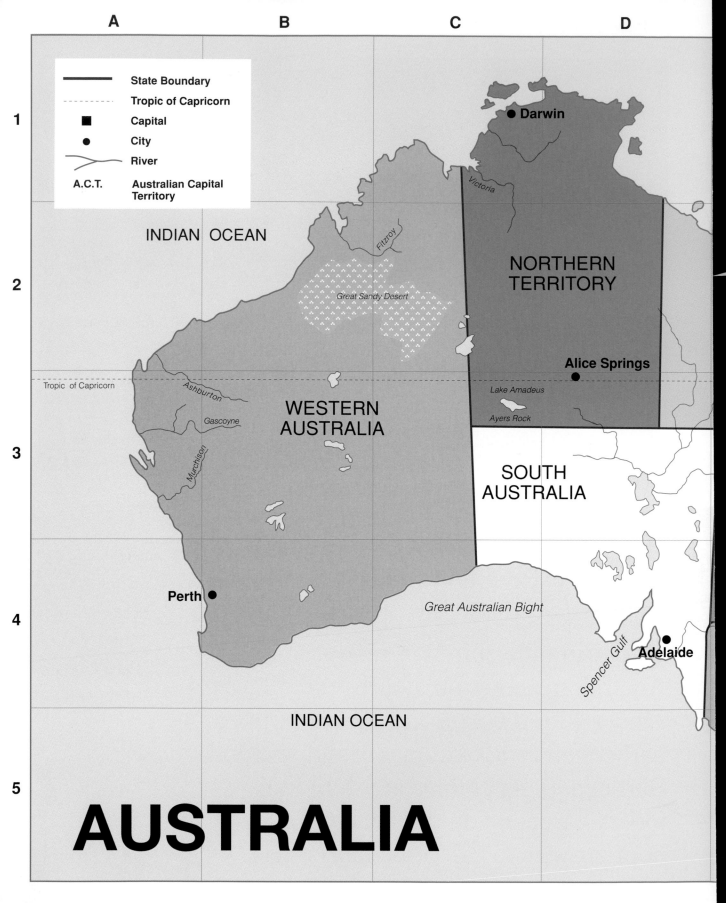

AUSTRALIA

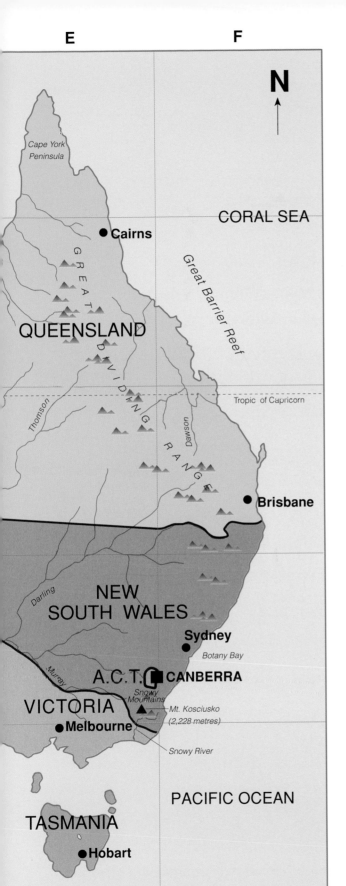

Adelaide D4
Alice Springs D3
Amadeus, Lake C3
Ashburton River A3
Australian Capital
    Territory
    (A.C.T.) E4
Ayers Rock C3

Botany Bay F4
Brisbane F3

Cairns E2
Canberra E4
Cape York
    Peninsula E1
Coral Sea F2

Darling River E4
Darwin C1
Dawson River F3

Fitzroy River C2

Gascoyne River B3
Great Australian
    Bight C4
Great Barrier Reef F2
Great Dividing Range
    E2–F3
Great Sandy
    Desert B2

Hobart E5

Indian Ocean A2–B5

Lachlan River E4

Melbourne E5
Mount Kosciusko E4
Murchison River A3
Murray River E4

New South Wales E4
Northern Territory C2

Pacific Ocean F5
Perth B4

Queensland E2

Snowy Mountains F5
Snowy River F5
South Australia C3–D3
Spencer Gulf D4
Sydney F4

Tasmania E5
Thomson River E3
Tropic of Capricorn A3

Victoria E4
Victoria River C1

Western Australia B3

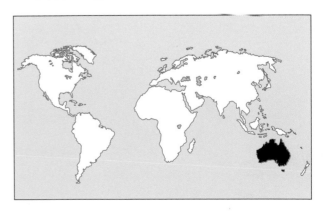

Quick Facts

Official Name   Australia

Capital   Canberra

Official Language   English

Population   19,913,144 (July 2004 estimate)

Land Area   7,682,000 square kilometres

States   New South Wales, Queensland, South Australia, Tasmania, Victoria, Western Australia

Territories   Australian Capital Territory, Northern Territory

Major Cities   Adelaide, Brisbane, Cairns, Canberra, Darwin, Melbourne, Perth, Sydney

Highest Point   Mount Kosciusko 2,228 metres

Major River   Murray River

Main Religions   Anglican 26.1 per cent, Catholic 26 per cent

Major Festivals   Australia Day (26 January)

ANZAC Day (25 April)

Christmas (25 December)

National Animals   Emu, kangaroo

Currency   Australian dollar (AUD $1.69 = £1 in July 2004)

Opposite: This sign warns that camels, wombats or kangaroos may be crossing ahead.

Glossary

Aborigines: the original people of Australia.

boomerang: a *V*-shaped hunting weapon used by the Aborigines.

bush: an area of forest, desert or scrubland outside the main cities.

bush-walking: hiking in the bush.

cabinet: group of government ministers.

constellation: a group of stars forming patterns in the sky.

convicts: people who are serving a prison sentence.

damper: a dumpling made from flour, sugar and water.

"down under": another name for the country of Australia.

federation: a group of governmental organisations.

fleece: a sheep's coat.

immigrants: people who live in a country they were not born in.

kebabs: chunks of meat and vegetables on skewers or wrapped in bread.

marsupials: animals whose young babies live in the mother's pouch.

multi-culturalism: including many different countries and cultures.

New Holland: the former name of Australia.

outback: the central area of Australia.

Passover: a Jewish festival held in spring.

policy: a strategy or rule made by the government.

prime minister: the political leader of a country.

rural: relating to the countryside, away from towns and cities.

Southern Hemisphere: the southern half of Earth.

sporting ovals: fields built for sports activities and competitions.

temperate: having a climate with four seasons.

tropical: having a climate with hot, sticky, wet weather all year round.

United Kingdom: the collective name for England, Scotland, Wales and Northern Ireland.

veteran: a former soldier.

witchetty grub: a small, white, slug-like creature.

More Books to Read

Australia and the Pacific. Malcolm Potter and Keith Lye (Evans Publishing Group)

Australia, Country File series. Dana Meachen Rau (Franklin Watts)

Australia. Letters from Around the World series. Margot Richardson (Evans Publishing Group)

Australia. Nations of the World series. Robert Darlington (Raintree)

Australia, Take Your Camera. Ted Park (Raintree)

Australia. World Tour series. Leigh Ann Cobb (Raintree)

Changing Face Of: Australia. Margot Richardson (Hodder Wayland)

Living in Australia. David Hampton (Franklin Watts)

Videos

Exploring Tropical Australia. (Rand McNally)

In The Wild – Australia. (Start Audio and Video)

Web Sites

library.thinkquest.org/28994/index.html

www.brisbane-stories.powerup.com.au/maggil/maggil_frames.htm

www.nationalgeographic.com/earthpulse/reef/reef1_flash.html

www.zoomschool.com/school/Australia/

Due to the dynamic nature of the Internet, some web sites stay current longer than others. To find additional web sites, use a reliable search engine with one or more of the following keywords to help you locate information about Australia. Keywords: *Aborigines, boomerangs, Great Barrier Reef, marsupials, outback, Sydney.*

Note to parents and teachers
Every effort has been made by the Publishers to ensure that these web sites are suitable for children; that they are of the highest educational value, and that they contain no inappropriate or offensive material. However, because of the nature of the Internet, it is impossible to guarantee that the contents of these sites will not be altered. We strongly advise that Internet access is supervised by a responsible adult.

Index

Aborigines 6, 10, 20, 26, 28, 30, 40
agriculture 12,18
ANZACs 13, 38
architecture 31
Australia Day 39
Australian Rules football 25, 34, 36
Ayers Rock 6

barbecues 38, 41
boomerangs 10
Brisbane 6, 13
bush-walking 35

Canberra 16
Carey, Peter 29
Cawley, Yvonne 37
Chisholm, Caroline 15
Christianity 26, 27
Christmas 38, 41
climate 5, 8, 9, 34
Cook, James 11

damper 41

farming 7, 12, 18
film 33
flag 5
Flinders, Matthew 15

food 40, 41
Freeman, Cathy 37

George III, King 11
Great Barrier Reef 7
Great Dividing Range 7

horse racing 36
House of Representatives 17
Howard, John 17

immigrants 12, 13, 14, 15, 20, 21, 27, 28, 39, 40
industry 18, 19

kangaroos 9
koalas 9

language 28
literature 29

manufacturing 18, 19
McCullough, Colleen 29
Melba, Nellie 32
Melbourne 6
Melbourne Cup 36
mining 12, 19
Mount Kosciusko 7

multiculturalism 21
Murray River 7
music 25, 31, 32

New Holland 15
Norman, Greg 37

opossums 9
outback 6, 29, 41

painting 30
Perth 6

Rafter, Pat 37

schools 24, 25
Senate 17
Southern Cross 5
sports 25, 34, 36, 37
Sutherland, Joan 32
Sydney 6, 11, 14, 21, 27, 31, 32, 40
Sydney Harbour Bridge 31
Sydney Opera House 31

White, Patrick 29
Wimbledon 37
World War I 13
World War II 13, 14